The Art of Archi
Modelling in Paper

T. A. Richardson

Alpha Editions

This Edition Published in 2021

ISBN: 9789355890306

Design and Setting By
Alpha Editions
www.alphaedis.com
Email – info@alphaedis.com

TABLE OF CONTENTS

FRONTISPIECE.

PREFACE

In offering the following practical dissertation (the first ever yet published) upon the Art of Architectural Modelling, the Author feels that he is supplying a want that must have been long felt by many students and others in the architectural profession. The utility of the "Model," coupled with its beauty, is ample recommendation of the study; and the modeller will be able to furnish the architect with sure and certain means that he may find weighty difficulties surmounted, especially in the case of uncomprehending clients, by giving to them the designs of their edifices with a distinctness almost equal to the real work when completed. With many clients, even "perspectives" are poorly understood, which seldom fails to cause some slight dissatisfaction on their part when they see too late certain things that the eye would have detected in the model and corrected in the outset. Models are becoming very general, where buildings are subjects of competition; and as this course of procedure and honourable encounter bids fair (when weeded of some of its present objections) to open up a good and honourable system, whereby the "race *may be* to the swift," the importance of the following brief and simple Treatise on the subject, becomes doubly clear.

T. A. R.

CHESTER, *March, 1859.*

INTRODUCTION.

The art of Architectural Modelling is not so difficult to acquire, as an observer, examining a model and admiring the minuteness of its parts, would be led to suppose. But in order to gain a certain degree of proficiency, a large amount of patience and perseverance is absolutely necessary. The great beauties of a model consist, firstly, in perfect symmetry and correctness of parts, all the angles being clear, well-defined, and sharp, the various minutiæ of detail accurately delineated; and secondly, to the straightness and evenness of the horizontal and perpendicular lines. It will be, therefore, readily understood, that it is these portions of the manipulation which demand the student's attention, more particularly as the joining of the paper or cardboard by means of a mitre, as well as the cutting of lines on the slant in either a horizontal or curved direction, is somewhat difficult. These difficulties which arise in the student's path are, however, easily to be overcome, and he must not grow faint-hearted if, after repeated trials, he does not succeed in producing the required effect. Rather at this juncture let him examine some model by an adept in the art, comparing his work with it. By these means he will be enabled to see the points in his own requiring improvement, and then let him continue to labour perseveringly and diligently until he gains a perfect command of his knife and materials, and few will be found but will admit that the result at last obtained fully repays him for his time and labour. There is no doubt that the art is of very great antiquity, and that in former times no building of importance was erected without one having been previously constructed. This not only aided the successful carrying out of the architect's drawings, but enabled him and his employer to judge better as to the general effect the work would have when completed.

We have mention made of models as early as 1546, when San Gallo (a pupil of Bramante, the original architect of St. Peter's, at Rome), either himself constructed, or caused to be, a model of his proposed designs for that magnificent structure, in order that the whole might be carried out in the same spirit in the event of his death. On this latter event occurring, the immortal Michael Angelo Buonarotti undertook the important office of architect to St. Peter's. One of his first tasks was to set aside the model of his predecessor, which had occupied many years in constructing, at a cost of many thousand pounds, while he constructed himself, at a trifling expense and in a few days, another model of his intended work. Numerous other instances of the practical utility of this branch of art might be cited, but the author deems it unnecessary, its importance being at once obvious; and this little work, though devoid of all technicalities, too frequently the fault of works of this description, yet is intended shall be eminently practical. To a large and increasing body, the architectural assistants, it is hoped that this little hand-book will prove to be acceptable; and though written principally for the professional man, it is hoped it may not prove utterly useless or uninteresting to others, who though not members of the architectural profession may yet possess sufficient taste and skill to wish to perpetuate

A DESIGN IN PAPER.

PART I.
OF THE MATERIALS REQUIRED.

The materials the architectural modeller will require for his work, are, for the most part, few, simple, and inexpensive. They are also easily procured at any of the Artists' Repositories. It is not, therefore, so much in the material employed, but in the skill displayed in the working, that the beauties of a model consist. The principle in this description of modelling being, that every possible part be constructed of paper, it is necessary that this should be procured of the description best suited to the nature of the work, and of the best possible quality. Inferior papers are hard, contain knots and other imperfections, and are very frequently gritty; this latter imperfection, by destroying the delicate edge of the knife, prevents the work having that sharp appearance so much to be desired. The paper I use, and have always found the best for all purposes, has a surface similar to that of Whatman's double-elephant drawing paper, and is, I believe, sold under the name of Crayon paper: a specimen is bound with this book, forming the *next page*; it is of a pale cream-colour, bearing a strong semblance in tint to Bath-stone, but I have procured it from this to the shades necessary for the roofs of models. It is firm, though not hard, in texture, and not being too spongy, does not absorb to too great a degree the paste used in fastening together the sheets for the various thicknesses required, thus ensuring their firmness, a matter of the highest importance, otherwise in thin strips consisting of four, five, or more thicknesses of paper, upon their being cut each would part and defeat the desired end.

The most useful tint of this paper is the one already described, as it can be easily tinted to represent bricks or rubble, &c., should it be necessary,—for instance, in a building where the quoins, dressings, &c., were in stone, the rest in random rubble or brick, it would enable you to mark them with a HHH pencil, and tint before your work was made up. I have constructed several models in pure white Bristol board, but it is a tedious hard material to work in, though the result is very fine.

The next most important auxiliary is an adhesive material for fastening the sheets together to produce the necessary thicknesses of cardboard, and to fix the whole together and the several parts in their places. For the former a paste of flour made in the following manner, will be found to be the best. To every two tablespoonfuls of the best wheaten flour, add a teaspoonful of common moist or brown sugar, and a little corrosive sublimate, the whole to be boiled, and while boiling continually stirred to prevent lumps, till of the right consistency. If a few drops of some essential oil, say lavender or peppermint, be added, the usual mouldiness will not appear, and the paste will keep for a great length of time. For the latter, a gum must be used, prepared by the following proportions. To each six ounces of the best gum arabic, add an ounce or less of moist or lump sugar, one teaspoonful of lavender or other essential oil, and a table-spoonful of gin, the whole to be mixed in *cold* water (no heat being in any way applied) to the consistency of a thick syrup.

Other requisites are sheets of mica or talc, to be procured at the ironmonger's, and used for windows, skylights, &c.; pieces of soft deal or beech wood, to form any small detail such as pinnacles to barge boards, &c., that it may not be advisable or possible to form in paper; wire, lead, cord, velvet, and numerous other nick-nacks, which will occur to the modeller as his work proceeds, and which will hereafter, in their place, be carefully described.

PART II.
OF THE INSTRUMENTS
NECESSARY.

The first thing the artist must procure must be a board of fine, close-grained wood, free from knots, to prepare and cut the several parts of his work upon. The best for this cutting-board is beech, sycamore, or pear-tree wood; it should be, at the least, one and a-half inch thick, by twelve inches broad, and about eighteen inches in length. I should prefer it even thicker than stated, as continual planing of the surface to erase the marks of the knife soon reduces its thickness. Let it be squared perfectly every way to allow the T square to work accurately along its edge. As before stated, care must be taken, when the surface has become too much cut up, to have it re-planed, or otherwise the knife is apt to follow the marks in the board, and cut the paper irregularly upon the under side. The size of board mentioned will be found most useful for all ordinary purposes; should the work be of very large dimensions, of course another must be procured, proportionally larger. Two or three boards of close-grained deal will also be found of service for cutting obliquely, &c., &c.

THE MODELLING PRESS.

This apparatus will be found of essential service to the artist, as by its aid he forms the cardboard which is the basis of his model. It may be either of iron or wood; the former is lighter, and more elegant in appearance, but the latter, though plain and homely, is in my opinion preferable in many respects. A common copying press may be used, care being taken not to place the damp paper between the iron, but between two hard, close-grained pieces of wood. On page 27 is an illustration of the press I use, which any joiner can construct for a few shillings. It consists of a cross-beam, A, through which the screw passes; two uprights, B B; a bottom, C, to which, and to the cross-beam, the uprights must be firmly mortised. Between them is a moveable top-piece, D, which by means of cord running through two small pulleys, E E, keeps it pressing continually against the screw; the weight F, at the end of the cord being slightly heavier than will balance the top-piece. By these means, as you unwind the screw, either to place under, or look at the progress of work already there, the top-piece moves out of your way. The sizes of the wood for the different portions is given, and care must be observed in not breaking it by too great a pressure of the screw; as the object of the press is to keep the sheets flatly and firmly together, while the adhesive material sets, no undue degree of force is necessary; indeed it will, for reasons hereafter to be described, be found a disadvantage to press them too closely.

THE MODELLING PRESS.

SIZES.

C	Bottom piece	18	inches	by	12	inches	by	2	inches.
B B	Uprights	12	do.	—	4	do.	—	1½	do.
A	Cross beam	15	do.	—	4	do.	—	2¼	do.

The screw 1⅜ths inch in diameter.

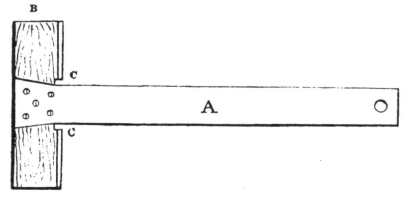

THE T-SQUARE.

This square is formed like the ordinary drawing-squares, with the exception that the blade A is made of steel; this is firmly screwed to a stock of hard wood, which has on each side of the blade a small piece at C C cut out; the object of this is to allow the knife to cut completely to the edge of the paper. The advantage, in fact, the necessity for a steel blade, will be obvious; were it of wood, the pressure of the knife along its edge would indent, or cut it. This square will be found adapted for every description of large and small work, but should the cardboard be of great thickness it is apt to stir, and by so doing cause irregularity of line. To remedy this an instrument is used, called an adjusting straight-edge. A is a straight ruler of flat brass, or of steel, like the blade of the T-square. It is contrived to move to and from the surface of the board upon the upright screws, B B, while a dovetail groove is fitted with a piece of brass to run along it, to allow of the horizontal movement of the ruler. The paper (upon which the cutting-off line has been previously marked) is placed upon the board, the straight-edge adjusted to the line; the straight-edge being then firmly screwed down upon it by means of the two small thumb-screws, 3 3, it is rendered immoveable during the progress of the work, this will be better understood from the annexed engraving.

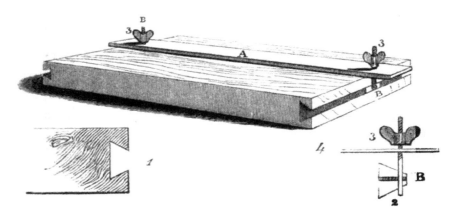

THE ADJUSTING STRAIGHT-EDGE.

No. 1 is a section of the cutting-board, showing the groove in which the piece of brass runs. 2, The brass, to which is attached the thumb-screws, by means of a screw through the eye at B. 3 3 3, Thumb-screws, to screw down the ruler upon the paper. The brass rule should not be less than an eighth of an inch in thickness, otherwise it may bend; if steel it will do a little less.

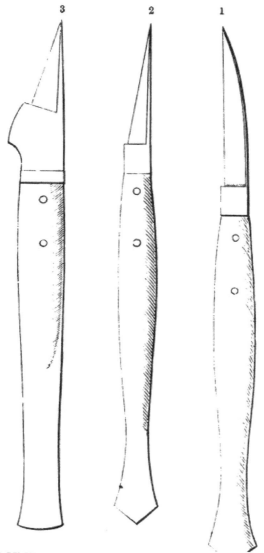

MODELLING KNIVES.

This instrument will be found particularly useful in cutting the necessary mitres for joining together the edges of the work, or for any other work of similar description, such as the copings to walls, mouldings of every description, &c., &c. Having now described these very important instruments in a way we hope may prove perfectly intelligible, we proceed to state the requirements in those necessary ones, knives. The number of these the artist will use, is regulated more by his own fancy than anything else; but there are three shapes he will find absolutely necessary. In modelling, as in painting, there are numerous tricks and contrivances for producing various effects; and as the painter will often value a bit of old scrubby, worn-down brush, so the modeller will find various cutting instruments materially assist him, such as the broken blade of a knife, a steel pen, a bradawl, &c., &c., many of these producing effects that more elaborate instruments would have failed doing. On page 33 will be found an engraving representing three requisite varieties of knives. No. 1. This knife is long in the blade, and, as will be found in all the others, is perfectly straight on the cutting edge; this knife is used to cut straight lines in all directions through strong work, cutting oblique lines, mitres, splays, &c. No. 2. One for lighter work used in forming or modelling ornaments, or, in general, cutting work of a lighter and neater character. No. 3. This blade is used solely for cutting all descriptions of circular work, and curves of every description. It may be useful to remark that this is the only shape of blade that will cut, with clearness and sharpness, curved lines through thick cardboard. The instrument next illustrated is called a knife compass, and is extremely valuable for cutting out circular architraves, &c., &c., doing its work in a way that the hand and knife could not equal, and with the least possible trouble. See illustration, page 36. They resemble, in some respects, an ordinary pair of compasses, but of a little stronger make than the common. A is a moveable sweep of brass, to regulate the opening of the legs of the compasses, which, being opened to the requisite width, are firmly held by tightening the thumb-screw, F. B, the moveable leg to which the cutting-knife C is attached by means of a shoulder to the blade at G, and a socket at H, into which it fixes, and is secured by the screw at D. E and I are two screws working on the rod, K, on each side of the moveable bar, B.

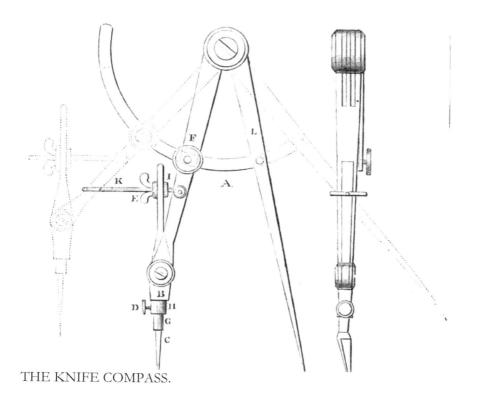

THE KNIFE COMPASS.

By means of this contrivance the knife is always kept perfectly upright, and in consequence cuts perpendicularly through the cardboard. There may be several knives to fit in the socket for light and heavy work, but a blade of the same shape as that shown in the engraving, will be found sufficient for nearly every purpose. The instrument might perhaps be more useful if half as large again as represented. The dotted lines are given to show the instrument open wider, in order fully to illustrate the utility of the moveable leg at B. The method of using this instrument is this: Having a curve to cut, and having found the centre of the arc, place the point of the leg L within it, then adjusting the moveable leg to the perpendicular by means of the screws I and E, stretch the legs to the requisite radius, and by gradually increasing the pressure on the blade, the curve may be cut with the most perfect ease and truth.

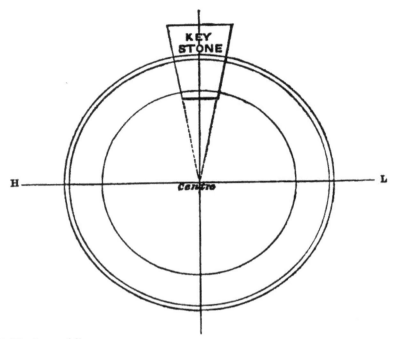

H L Horizontal line.

PART III.
THE COMMENCEMENT AND
FINISH OF A MODEL.

Assuming that the student has now procured the various instruments and materials for his work, and that he has also determined upon the design he intends in paper, the next thing necessary is to give him as far as it is possible by a book copiously illustrated, an exact description of the method of proceeding. We will therefore imagine a design which is to be modelled (see frontispiece), a Villa, in the domestic Italian style, for example; and taking it to pieces bit by bit, endeavour to raise it up again in renewed beauty and effect.

Having the four elevations, together with the ground and roof plans, the latter being essential to show the position of the chimneys, skylights, &c., we take a common drawing-board, about the size of the intended model, and upon it strain as for a drawing that size, a piece of drawing cartridge, say an inch and a half wider all round than the intended model is to be. Upon this, when dry, draw an *outline plan* of the intended building, not putting in any internal walls, for these will not be required as this is only to form lines whereon to erect the intended building. To make it more readily to be understood we have given a sketch of the outline plan on page 45.

15

ELEVATIONS OF VILLA.

ELEVATION OF ENTRANCE.

SIDE ELEVATION.

This being completed, we have now the edifice, as it were, set out. The next matter for consideration is the thickness of the walls; that is, the requisite thickness of paper we shall require. Suppose we take, as in the plan given, the outside reveal or recess back of the window frame, at four inches and a half; this would require four sheets of paper, but as it is always better to exaggerate slightly in modelling both projections and recesses, place six or even seven sheets together; paste them together in twos, putting them as pasted under the press, and afterwards, when nearly dry, paste them the full thickness required and subject them once more to the action of the press. The most convenient size of paper to work at for an ordinary-sized model will be made by doubling a sheet of the paper as first procured into four. On the paper becoming perfectly dry, the student must carefully draw each elevation of the building the full height from the ground line to the top of the blocking, being particular that every line both perpendicular and horizontal is perfectly true and square, and marking along faintly the lines for the cornice, strings, &c., &c., that may occur. This being done and the whole drawn in, of course not drawing in the window frames but merely the outline of the square of the window, the side will present the appearance shown in the accompanying elevation, and which is merely sketched and not drawn to any scale.

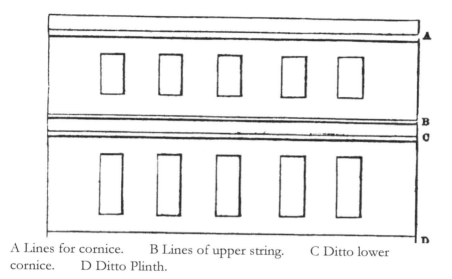

A Lines for cornice.　　B Lines of upper string.　　C Ditto lower cornice.　　D Ditto Plinth.

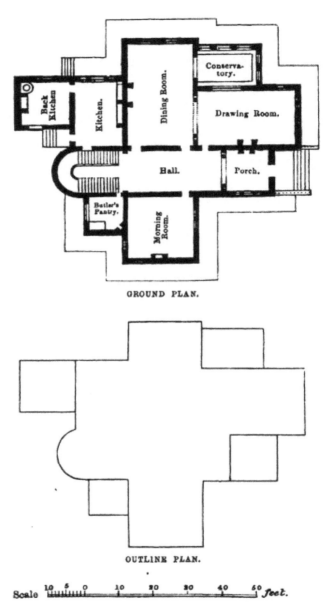

GROUND PLAN.

OUTLINE PLAN.

Scale ⊥⊥⊥⊥⊥⊥⊥⊥ 10 5 0 | 10 | 20 | 30 | 40 | 50 *feet.*

PLANS OF VILLA.

GROUND PLAN.

OUTLINE PLAN.

The four or more elevations having been drawn, proceed to cut out all windows, doors, and other openings cleanly and accurately. The windows and their frames must now be made and gummed at the back of the several openings; where panels occur paper of the same tint must be used, sometimes the pieces cut from the windows will form very good backing for such parts. For the window frames take some large-sized cream laid paper, and colour it to the tint you wish your frames to be. Should a representation of oak be preferred, it may be imitated successfully thus: First paint your paper yellow, gamboge and a little burnt sienna will do, and then prepare a thick colour with Chinese white and burnt sienna; when the first colour is dry lay this last-mentioned on, and before *it* has time to dry grain it by means of a fine comb; a small tooth comb will answer best for this purpose, and if skilfully performed a most admirable imitation will be the result. Three or four thicknesses of paper (cream laid or other white paper) must then be pasted together, with the oak-coloured one upon the top, and submitted to the action of the press.

This paper being ready for use, take one of the pieces cut from the windows, and mark by it the size of the window-opening, then lightly draw the frames in and cut them out, if the white paper of the under sheets should show where cut through sectionally, touch it along with a little burnt sienna or brown colour. You must now tint another sheet of the same description of paper blue or neutral, not in an even tint, but carelessly and artistically leaving bright lights; this when pasted as for the oak-paper two or three thicknesses, will form the backing to the frames. Then place the frames face down, on them gummed a sheet of mica; on that again the blue backing; the whole then to be put in the press, care being taken not exhibit too much pressure, otherwise you will have the backing bulge out. It may, perhaps, be thought that these thicknesses of paper for the frames and backing are unnecessary, and that one might serve as well; but from experience I can assert, that unless this method be adopted, that flatness the work should have, will not be obtained. It may also be as well here to caution the reader against pressing with too great a degree upon the cardboard when it is under the action of the press. If too great a pressure is given, the cardboard will become so hard as to resist all efforts of the knife to cut through it. The paper usually presses to a little less than an inch, to a scale of one-eighth of an inch to the foot; so that six thicknesses or sheets of paper will answer for four and a half of brickwork or stonework. The doors will be formed first from two thicknesses[1] and backed with the same. This is for plainest description, but if mouldings are inserted in the panels, adopt the following:—

<u>1</u>. One thickness, two thicknesses, three thicknesses, and so forth, will be used throughout, to express the number of sheets to be pasted together.

DETAILS No. 1.

ELEVATION OF ENTRANCE DOOR.

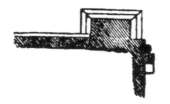 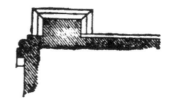

PLAN OF ENTRANCE DOOR.

First draw the door with the extreme size of the opening of each panel, on a two-thickness sheet; on another two-thickness sheet, draw the same panels a size smaller; on a third two-thickness sheet, draw them a size smaller still; these being cut out and placed behind one another, and finally the backing; will admirably represent mouldings: by producing three separate lines round the inside of each panel. For work to ⅛ scale no further trouble will be necessary; but if larger, the mouldings must be formed before the door is gummed together, as hereafter described for the formation of mouldings in general. The doors, windows, and backs to all openings are now ready, but cannot be yet fixed till all the necessary mitreing is completed, which mitres will be wherever an outside angle occurs thus, fig. 1. (See page <u>53</u>, figs. 1 and 2.)

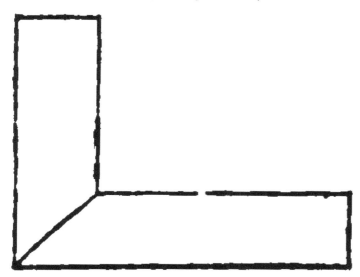

Fig. 1.

OUTSIDE ANGLE.

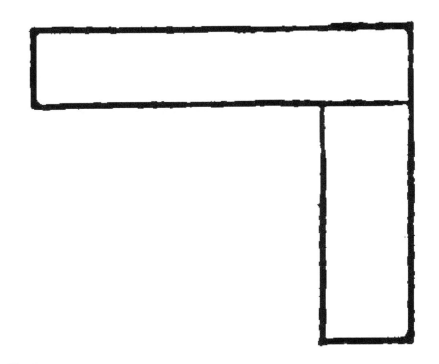

Fig. 2.

INSIDE ANGLE.

In the inner angle (see fig. 2) no mitre is required; the end of one piece being cut square, they may be made to overlap one another. Lay the piece, whatever it may be you wish to mitre, face down upon the cutting-board; and then at a distance (equal to the whole thickness of the cardboard) from the edge draw a line; and at a short distance back from this line sufficient to let the point of the knife touch it when held slanting to the required angle, fix the adjusting straight-edge previously described; screw firmly upon it, and cut through the paper at an angle of 45°, which will, of course, be by cutting from the line on the top side of the paper, A, to the extreme edge of the underside, B (see illustration page <u>55</u>), which represents the side of a building, and the piece may be seen curling up as cut from the mitre. Great steadiness of hand, and a few trials on waste cardboard are necessary before the operator will perform this skilfully. The straight-edge holding the paper firmly, it may be cut through at two or three strokes, observing to hold the knife always at the same angle. All mitreing work finished, affix the windows at the back, placing the whole under a slight pressure.[2] Then the model must be blocked up. First cut a number of squares, all sizes, from waste or other cardboard; let them be perfectly square; cut these diagonally, and they will form the blocks to hold the work together at the angles. Now take any two sides that are to be joined at the mitred angle, and fix them accurately together with gum pretty thick, so that it may dry while you hold each side in its place. When set, lay them down and work the others in a similar manner. Take now the outline plan, and having previously numbered the sides to correspond with the plan, fix them (by touching slightly their under edge with gum) to it, and when all are in their places fix, at a distance apart of an inch and half or so, above one another the previously described blocking pieces with gum not so thick in consistency. To make our meaning perfectly plain, we annex an engraving of the appearance of an internal angle when at this stage of the proceedings. A piece of wood (deal) about ½ inch thick, should now be attached to the model from one side to the other (see page <u>57</u>). This is for the purpose of fastening the model, when completed, to its stand; it may be blocked with waste pieces, such as the cuttings from doors, windows, &c., and gummed firmly. Pieces or strips of cardboard should also be gummed along in the inside, at the level of the intended gutters of the house, to rest the roof upon. All portions of the work completed, we will now assume, are fitted together and in their places. The student will now be able to form some idea of the general effect his work will have when finished; but there is yet more—much more—to be done, and work requiring a still further amount of skill, practice, and patience.

<u>2</u>. As there are many little matters during the progress of a model requiring a slight pressure, a pressure sufficient to hold the pieces in their several places till dry, I have found weights answer very well. I have pieces of square lead from one pound upwards covered with paper; and by covering, the humble brick may be usefully pressed into this service.

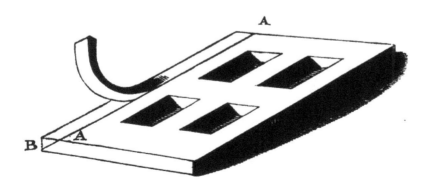

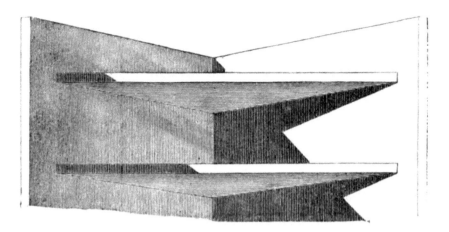

SKETCH SHOWING THE WAY THE BLOCKING PIECES ARE
INSERTED IN AN INTERNAL ANGLE.

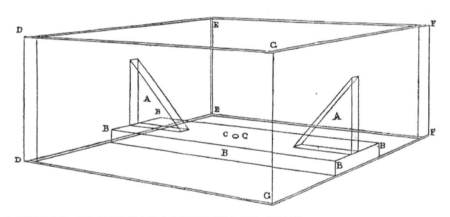

METHOD OF INSERTING THE WOOD STAY.

A A Cardboard angle stays.   B B B B B Wood stay by which the model is
affixed to its stand by a screw passing through at C C.   D E F G Sides of
model.

The two principal elevations are given to the same scale as the plan (page
41); but in order to insure our being understood, the principal portions of
the details are given to a larger scale.

The cornice next demands our attention, a detail of which is given on page 61, fig. 1, and in order to model which we proceed thus, the numbers indicating the various pieces of which it is composed. No. 2 is a piece worked of the required thickness demanded by the depth of the cornice from A to B, and the necessary projection, in a sufficient series of lengths to go entirely round the building. Now, as this is to be cut through the several thicknesses of paper required, a method must be found out to hide the different layers that would consequently be exposed to view; this is by cutting from one or two thicknesses a piece the whole length of the cornice, forming a facia, 8, and coming slightly below the depth of the other under piece to 4; thus, while at the same time it hides the layers of paper, it forms the bed of the cornice.

The next members, Nos. 1, 3, 5, and 7, are formed, first by preparing the size and length on the square; secondly, by cutting off at any angle necessary to get as near to the mould as possible; and, lastly, forming the mould itself.

The manner of moulding being applicable to every description of either Italian or Gothic pattern, we proceed to describe it.

Procure from the comb-manufacturers some pieces of *ivory* of various sizes, and with different files, some round, some square, &c., file on one end of a square piece the *reverse* of the mould you require; smooth it well; and for greater power and convenience, fix it in a handle of wood.

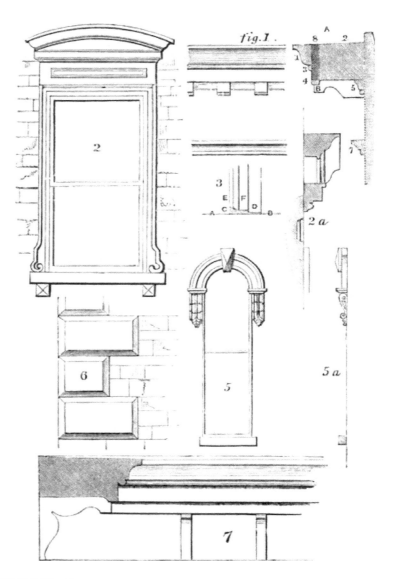

DETAILS No. 2.

1 Elevation and section of main cornice.   2 Elevation of window.   2a
A detail of section through window.   3 Architrave mould.   5
Elevation of small window.   5a Section of small window.   6
Elevation of quoins.   7 Section and elevation of tower cornice.

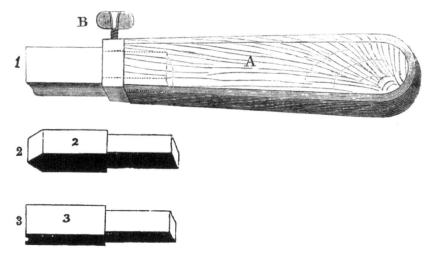

MOULDING TOOLS.

A, Handle with socket to secure the moulding tool (1).   B, Thumb-screw.   1, 2, 3, Moulding tools.

Nos. 1, 2, 3, &c., &c., will be found generally available and useful in the formation of all kinds of mouldings, besides numbers of other shapes that will occur to the artist. The method of using the instrument is by indenting the pattern along the edge of the cardboard, guided by means of the straight-edge. The sharp arris left from the file upon the edge of the ivory mould, had better be slightly taken off, to prevent the paper being torn in its passage.

The circular pediment over windows (fig. 2, page 61) must be modelled on the flat, and the moulding returned at the ends. When each member is finished, they must be gummed up and bent to the required curve, over a circle of cardboard or a cylinder of wood, separately. The panels that occur form thus: Cut as before directed for doors, the extreme size of the opening, and at the back place the successive sizes and thicknesses to form the mouldings, indented into hollows or worked to rounds, &c., &c., by means of one or more of the moulding tools; to be backed last of all.

Commence the preparation of the quoins (fig. 6, p. 61) by cutting pieces the required thickness and width of both long and short quoins, and in long strips, with the *height* of each one marked up its length previously by the dividers.[3] Cut first the requisite splay at the edge of the quoin, along the whole length both sides. Cut where marked for height, and splay top and bottom. They are then finished, and may be at once fastened to the work.

3. The small hair dividers, with the adjusting screw, will be found extremely useful in modelling work.

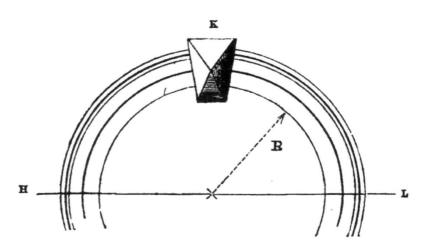

CIRCULAR ARCHITRAVES.

K Keystone.   R Radius.   H L Horizontal line.

The circular architraves must be formed by cutting, with the little instrument previously described as a knife-compass (page 36), circles of different diameters and thicknesses of paper suited to the mould to be represented; gum together while in the circle, as shown below, the horizontal divisional line being marked, and the radiating lines for the insertion of the keystones. When dry cut off by the divisional line, and then the segments, by the lines at each side of the keystone. The key must be of paper sufficiently thick to allow of the highest mould of the architrave abutting against it, and either left plain, cut diamond-wise, or carved, or any other way the fancy may suggest or the design demand.

The cantalivers in tower (fig. 7, page 61) and main cornices (fig. 1, page 61) to be worked by preparing paper the required thickness; then procuring a piece of very thin copper or lead, mark on it with considerable accuracy the design of the cantaliver, and cut it out; you will thus have prepared a mould or templet, which you can place upon the cardboard, and by running a hard pencil round it, mark each one precisely the same in size.

Any portions of the dressings, &c., having curves in them, had better be cut with knife No. 3[4]; in fact, this is the only shape of blade which will leave the edge of a curved line after cutting, what is technically called "sweet."

4. In using this knife, care must be taken to hold it perfectly upright, nor lean it either to right or left.

The positions the cantalivers have to occupy along the cornice, must be checked along and regularly divided. Care must also be taken in gumming them in their places, as one out of place or leaning would immediately be detected by a correct eye, and mar completely the effect of the whole.

The architrave mould (fig. 3, page 61) next demands our attention. It will from our former description be readily understood that all mouldings are formed by representing in paper of various thicknesses their several component parts. Thus, in the mould last named, we have first the groundwork of or thickness from A to B; another thickness, forming the sinking, from C to D; and finally, the mould, E to F. Square first, the required slant next cut from the edge, and lastly, the slant hollowed by means of one of the ivory moulding tools. The keystones and the blocks under the window sills are cut from paper the thickness required, then splayed down each way from the centre to the sides at *one* cut, and with a sharp knife. This operation must be performed with some dexterity, as it is important that the edges should be sharp and free from woolliness. This effect can only be obtained by giving one cut or slice in the direction required: for this purpose use knife No. 1, which will be found the best for this description of work. Some modellers use for this purpose a thin chisel with a keen edge; and of course all means in art are legitimate that produce the desired end; but we would recommend the use of the knife only, wherever possible, the modeller's object being to work with as few tools as possible, and to trust much to his knife alone.

DETAILS OF WINDOWS. No. 3.

MORNING ROOM.

KITCHEN.

We have, in describing the method of working several important details connected with the building, and illustrated on page 61, been, we fear, somewhat premature, and have not sufficiently urged upon the student the necessity of preparing his groundwork for these details in a perfectly accurate manner. For, as it is well known, no colouring, however fine, will in a picture make up for bad and incorrect drawing, so in a model, walls out of square or windows and other apertures ill-cut will not present the wished-for appearance, though all the details be most skilfully and beautifully modelled. Draw in all doors, windows, &c., &c., with a very hard pencil, in order that the lines may be as fine as possible, and cut them out with knife No. 1, or No. 2, whichever may be considered most suitable to the size of opening it is required to cut; the knife No. 3, as before observed, being used exclusively for curved and circular work. In cutting out the windows, hold your knife perfectly upright; and, as you arrive at the end of the cut, let the *edge* of the blade be perpendicular, thus avoiding cutting past the line. In cutting through thick, or indeed even through one thickness of paper, do not be too anxious to sever the piece with one cut, as this way of proceeding is almost sure to cause unevenness of line. But commence by *drawing* a line, as it were, in the required direction; that the rule may guide it accurately, press but slightly at first; and as the track of the knife gets deeper, exert more pressure. Simple as this direction may appear, it is nevertheless of the utmost practical utility, as will readily be found upon trial, as it is only by these means that the paper will be left at the edge clean, sharp, and even.

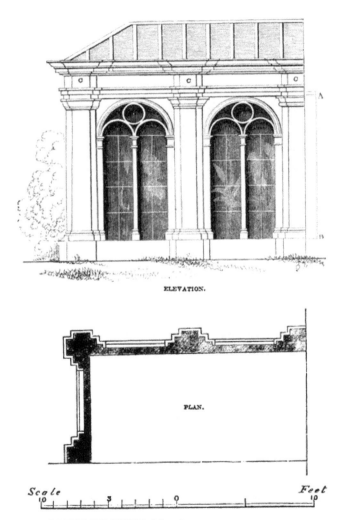

ELEVATION.

PLAN.

Scale   *Feet*

DETAILS OF GREENHOUSE. No. 1.

The next object we would call attention to is the Greenhouse, page 73, and state that there are two ways of modelling this very general appendage to a modern mansion. The first and the simplest method is to form the backing of blue paper behind the mica. The other, by doing away with the blue backing, and allowing the mica to remain transparent. The former method saves some amount of labour; but the latter being in our opinion the best and most artistic method, we shall proceed to describe it: First form the pilasters (you will require double the number than for the opaque backing), and cut them in their length from A to B (see elevation, page 73), from the commencement of the base mouldings to the underside of those of the cap. The way of proceeding in modelling cap and base will be readily understood from the accompanying sketch, where it will at once be seen better than we can describe. The best way to cut them is as if they were a window or opening, cutting the piece out of the centre at A, after having moulded the edge all round. Then dividing them into two along the line D L as below, fix them in their respective places. The angle ones must be double, to avoid having to mitre them. A piece of mica or thin glass cut to the size of the one side is now taken, and the pilasters and other portions, divisional bars, &c., are gummed to it, on both sides; and when with the end it is finished, let it occupy its intended position on the outline plan.

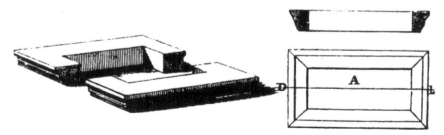

D L Divisional line.

Now proceed to the roof, to be constructed really of iron and glass, to be modelled of paper and mica: First, bend round a paper or other cylinder the piece of mica for the roof, and proceed to cut a number of strips of cardboard for the ribs, which may be coloured any suitable tint.

DETAILS OF GREENHOUSE. No. 2.

PART ELEVATION.
Scale   ¼ inch one foot.

These are then to be affixed in their places, as shown upon the drawing, some in thicker, others in thinner paper. A ledge of cardboard must be left at the back of the blocking, and also on the same level against the side of the house; this will be for the purpose of resting the roof upon.[5] The cornice will be constructed in the manner described for the others; the pieces on the frieze C, C, C (page 73) will be placed on the required thickness for the return, but the return of the cornice must be cut in it. The plinth must now be moulded, cut, and fixed; and the whole is complete.

5. This description is for a circular roof; that, however, in the engraving represents a flat hipped roof. The method of proceeding is the same, except that for the latter no cylinder is required.

Chimneys, those great ornaments to a house, at least they should be rendered so, but, alas! for the taste of some of our modern architects, are far more frequently the reverse, and what in able hands and with judicious treatment would prove a crowning feature and a material assistance to the design, becomes a glaring error and ruins the whole. So much for the architect: but should he fortunately possess the ability and taste to produce those necessaries to our comfort, with equal credit to himself and benefit to the design, how often do we see his work marred by the introduction of Messrs. Somebody's patent never-failing revolving smoke preventer; a hideous monster of some seven feet high, whirling and screeching upon the slightest appearance of wind. As our little Handbook has its mission to instruct in the Art of Modelling an architect's production, and as smoke-jacks are but little indebted to him for their uneasy existence, we beg to apologise for this digression, and resume our original topic. Details of the chimneys will be found upon page 81 and 83; for the body of the chimney use two thicknesses, and it will not be found necessary to mitre the join; for, if even ordinary care be taken, the union will be scarcely perceptible, while the labour will be considerably diminished. Form any strings, cornices, &c., &c., that occur, by cutting the piece flat, and then cutting the square out of the middle to admit of the shaft, slip it over the shaft or body of the chimney, till it arrives at the position required by the design, where it is at once to be secured in its place. Perhaps our meaning may be rendered clearer by the accompanying illustration. A represents the cornice prepared in the manner described, and only requiring to be fixed in its place. B, the shaft or body of the chimney over which the cornice is to be slipped till it arrives at the dotted lines; the chimneys may be fixed to the roof (shortly to be described) in the following manner: Should the chimney come on the roof lower down than the ridge, the bottom of the shaft will have to be cut to the angle required by the rake of the roof only; but should the chimney be cut into by the ridge, then the angle will follow that of the roof on both sides, diverging from the apex. For illustration of this we give the annexed sketches, page <u>83</u>.

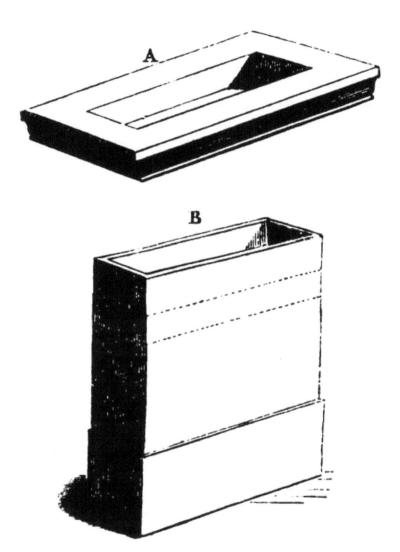

DETAILS OF CHIMNEYS.

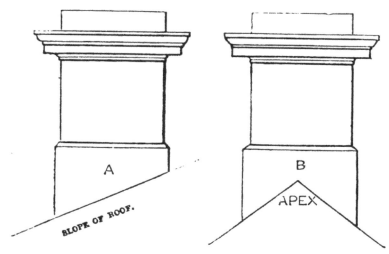

DETAILS OF CHIMNEYS.

A represents a chimney, the base of which is cut simply *one way*, to suit the slope of the roof. B, a chimney into which the ridge cuts, and the angle cut both ways from the apex. It will, as a general rule, be found better to put chimneys together with thin paper, even in the smallest models, a squareness being thus produced not to be obtained otherwise. The base to be formed out of thickness equal to the projection, and treated in (as regards fitting it to the roof) a similar manner to the shaft, so that if the rake of shaft had chanced not to have been truly cut, there is no need to throw it away, as it could easily be blocked under with small pieces till straight, the base hiding all defects underneath. The method of working the strings, cornices, &c., has already been fully described in those for the tower and main building. Figs. 1 and 7, page <u>61</u>.

Our model now draws near to its completion. We had arrived at a stage ready for the roof, but stopped for the preparation of the chimneys, in order that when the roof was completed, they might be at once fixed in their respective places. The roof may be either scored, or gauged with paper strips overlapped. The groundwork for either method will be prepared in the same manner. First cut, as if for a lid or top to fit the inside of the model, a strong piece of cardboard; let it be just so that it will slip into its place between the walls, but be prevented slipping down by the strips or ledge on the level of the gutter, as described for Greenhouse, page <u>73</u>.

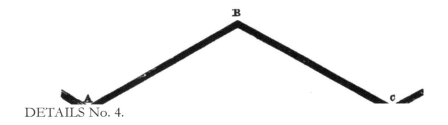

DETAILS No. 4.

Fig. 1.

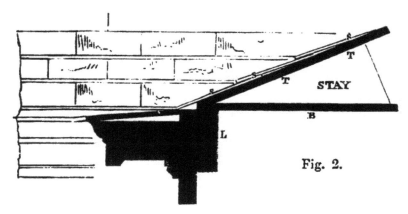

Fig. 2.

Fig. 2.

B Bottom piece.   C Cornice.   L Ledge.   S S S Slates.   T Top
piece.   W Wall.
The cross hatching shows the number of separate pieces the cornice is
composed of.

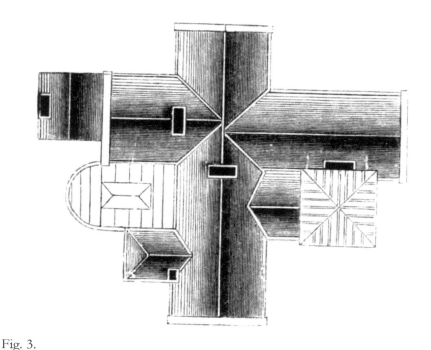

Fig. 3.

ROOF PLAN.

Sections must now be taken in various parts, through the roof, to ascertain the length of the respective sides. Thus if the angle A B C (see fig. 1, page 85) represents the rake of the roof, the length of the side will be found from A to B and B to C. The sides thus formed must be splayed to fit at the valleys, apex, &c., and at the base splayed and fixed to the top piece on which the roof plan has been drawn, observing to leave space enough all round for the gutter. If the pieces on which the sections have been drawn are cut out, they will answer for internal stays to the roof.

The roof plan is given upon page 85, fig. 3, as also an outline section for the finishing of the roof, fig. 2, page 85; it will explain itself. The lead flat will be formed by the bottom piece, but it must be covered by a paper resembling in tint that of the lead itself. When the groundwork of the roof is completed, it must be covered in imitation of slates by one or other of the previously-mentioned methods. We will, however, describe both, leaving the reader to use his own judgment as to which he may adopt, our preference being for the strips of overlapping paper. In the simple scoring, proceed to cut out of the slate tinted paper pieces accurately fitting to the groundwork of the roof, then with the knife handle score these sides along, as you would ink in the roof lines in a drawing, closer at the ridge, becoming wider at the base, and parallel to each other. The latter by cutting layers of paper, gauged decreasing in size as before directed, fixing them to the groundwork of the roof beginning at the base, and overlapping them about 1/16th of an inch; after all, submitting to the press. The roof assumed to be finished, affix the chimneys, generally make good all imperfections, &c., and the model is ready for removal to its final destination; cut therefore the paper it was built upon from the board, and also tear from the bottom edges the paper that may have adhered to it, holding it by the wood stay.

Prepare a piece of dry wood about two or three inches wider all round than the building itself, cover it with cloth or velvet, the latter preferable, the best colour green, and cut a small groove out of the upper edge; this is to receive the glass shade, which construct thus: procure five pieces of glass, the sizes rendered necessary by your stand to form a square or oblong shade, and fasten all together by means of strips of thin paper and gum (the dull gold paper to be procured in sheets at any of the artists' repositories will look best) at their edges. The model must now be secured to the stand, for which purpose the piece of wood mentioned at page 56 was inserted, a hole is drilled through the bottom of the stand, and a screw passed through it into the wood stay. Do not screw the model down too tightly upon the stand, or you may force away the stay from its fastenings and destroy your work.

We have now described all the necessary materials and manipulations to complete in every respect a model similar to the mansion given in the illustrations, and which, though containing the general detail of a building of that description, was wanting in numerous varieties of detail that will occur in many other buildings of the same class more ornate and considerably more elaborate in design than our example.

While all our attention is being turned towards Italian architecture, Gothic must not be forgotten, and though the general method of procedure is the same for both, yet there are numerous things which exist only in the latter style, and in consequence demand separate instructions. In order, therefore, that nothing shall escape being described in the various styles, that the student may have nothing to retard his operations, we append the methods of working the various details in the form of an illustrated glossary, the alphabetical arrangement of which will, we think, enable the student more readily and quickly to find the particular information he may require.

PART IV.
HINTS ON LANDSCAPE GARDENING; LAYING OUT GROUNDS, &C.

We have, as yet, proposed to finish the model in the plainest and most simple way, completely unaided and unadorned by the adjuncts of gardens or trees. And yet, that models are frequently considerably improved in appearance by these imitations of natural objects, when taste and skill go hand in hand, will be admitted by all, but we often see them completely spoiled by such additions. It is indeed somewhat difficult to say how far we may venture with propriety upon this path, and where to draw the line requires some tact; we will not, therefore, lay down any rule absolutely as to how far the laying out of grounds and the modelling of the trees, &c., may be admissible, only giving some instructions for modelling the objects themselves. And though the grounds are laid out, the picturesque undulations of the surface, the ponds, flower-beds, arcades, terraces, lawns, shrubs, and trees, faithfully represented, let it not for one moment be supposed that by so doing we render what was before a work of art, a mere toy. Far from it. We do not wish the reader, when he thinks of a model, to remember those of York Minster, or Strasbourg Cathedral, and which, borne aloft upon the shoulders of some wandering Italian, tempt the vulgar by the rich colours of the stained glass inserted in their chalk sides, and brilliantly illuminated by the light of a farthing candle placed within; or of the grounds, as bearing any resemblance to those interesting toys representing a *"castle in cork,"* about an inch high, whose clinging ivy is represented by one of the largest species of moss, and in whose luxurious gardens bloom roses two inches in diameter, roses which should have decked some matron's cap, but which for the nonce were pressed into this more noble service. But, to proceed. Balusters of grotesque, Elizabethan, or other patterns, when cut out of the solid stone, must be made by gumming the paper in different thicknesses, till that required is obtained, carefully drawing the pattern, and then cutting out with knife No. 3. Turned work, as circular pedestals for statues, sundials, gate-piers, balusters, &c., cannot be successfully imitated in paper, but are better turned in wood of some light colour, and then tinted with body colour to the required shade; all work of the same description that is *square* may be constructed in exactly the same manner as before described for chimney-stacks. For a representation of lawns and grassy slopes, meadow, &c., we may take white velvet, and tint it to any required shade, or use cloth which can be obtained any shade of green, or even flock paper may be procured, which, when cleverly laid on the work, gives an excellent imitation of grass; but of all these methods, velvet tinted will be found the most effective and best. Water, represent with looking-glass, or with mica, to the back of which is gummed paper of suitable tint for the situation of the water. For rocks, grottoes, &c., take stout white paper, and thoroughly soak it in water until it is rendered quite pliable, and then with the fingers, pieces of wood, or any thing that may suggest itself as being useful, mould or model it to the required shapes fancy or skill may suggest, and afterwards tint it to resemble nature. An effect better still may be obtained by gumming it, when perfectly dry, with thick gum, and then dusting or sprinkling it with fine sand, which may be procured of various shades. This method adopt also for walks, carriage-drives, or any place where a representation of road, or gravel, may be required. Cut out your flower-beds in thin cork, and then burn the upper surface; this will give the appearance of rich mould, or earth, and also serve as a good groundwork to stick the shrubs and flowers into. In your trees, rather aim at a general or suggestive effect, than at much minutiæ of detail; procure pieces of twigs, and shape them for the trunks and branches, and then gum on them the smallest-leaved moss, in good outline to represent nature; this moss will, when perfectly dried, bear tinting well. Flower-patches, the same moss with a bit of bright scarlet, or other paper, here and there gummed among it.

We have now given sufficient general instructions to enable the student to proceed with this branch, should his fancy lead him; and with these suggestions, and his own practice, he may in a short time be enabled to imitate successfully the quaint gardens of the Elizabethan period, or the more natural taste evinced in the landscape gardening of our own times.

... "Does airy fancy cheat

My mind well pleased with the deceit?

I seem to hear, I seem to move,

And wander through the happy grove,

Where smooth springs flow, and murmuring breeze

Wantons through the waving trees."

CREECH.

PART V.

A GLOSSARY

CONTAINING THE METHODS OF WORKING VARIOUS DETAIL, &C., NOT HITHERTO DESCRIBED.

A.

ARCH.—As a general rule, every description of arch may be successfully modelled by means of the knife-compass; each separate moulding that occurs must consist of separate pieces of paper, the edge of which has been moulded by one or other of the means described, and these layers gummed over one another when finished. To make our meaning clearer, in fig. 1 next page, a section of a cornice is given, as illustrating the method to be adopted for arches. It will here be seen that it is composed of six separate pieces, or, more properly speaking, thicknesses, for each portion will be made of the number of thicknesses required by its depth; No. 1, the fillet, square, No. 2, the cyma recta, first splay, as shown by the dotted line; and then press with the moulding tool to the required shape, and thus proceed with all the other members.

This cornice is not drawn to any scale.

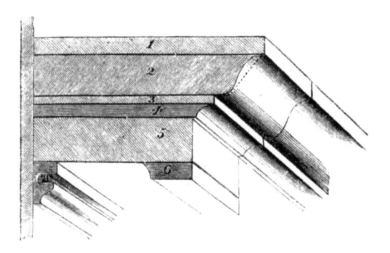

Fig. 1.

No. 1 Fillet.   No. 2 Cyma recta.   No. 3 Fillet.   No. 4 Casetto.
No. 5 Facia.   No. 6 Continuation of facia.   No. 7 Bed mould.

Where deep hollows occur, as in Gothic mouldings, a different method must be adopted, see fig. 2, the moulding for a Gothic window jamb; here the deep hollows are constructed by bending thin paper to the required curve, and gumming it in the right angles, or other angles required. A and B represent the outside walls of the work, and C C C C the various angles required by the mouldings. As will be seen, the other mouldings are formed on the ends of angle-pieces, in the same manner as adopted for the cornice.

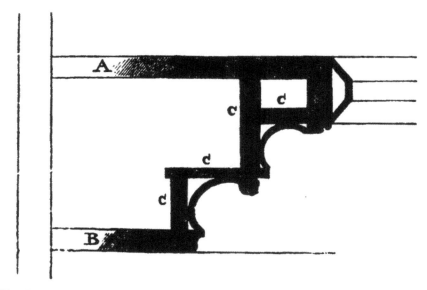

Fig. 2.

ARCHITRAVE.—In forming these, the same method may be adopted as for cornices, cutting the mouldings separately, and laying them one over the other in the order in which they come. Circular architraves are easily and beautifully cut with the knife-compass.

ACANTHUS.—The method of modelling the leaves of this plant, so much used in ornamentation, will be afterwards described under the general head of ornaments.

ASHLAR.—In representing work of two kinds, namely, quoins of dressed work, and filling in of random tooled ashlar:—Draw the quoins in with a H H H pencil, score in the ashlar, and tint as may be desired.

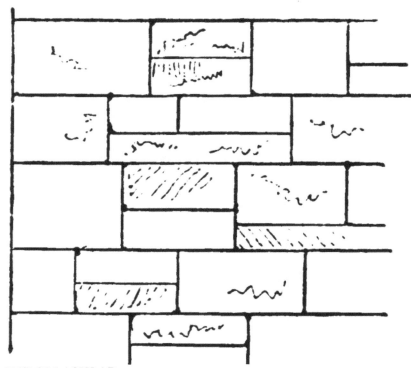

RANDOM ASHLAR.

ASTRAGAL.—First cut your paper square, thus—

next bevel the edge thus

and then, with one of the hollow ivory moulding tools run along the edge by pressure, give the intended round.

ACROTERIA.—May be modelled in exactly the same manner as previously described for chimney shafts (see page 80, *ante*).

B.

BARGE BOARD.—First determine on the thickness your board is to be, and then let the paper for it be pressed closer together than that used for ordinary work; carefully draw the pattern, and cut out with knife No. 3, splaying the tracery with knives Nos. 1 and 2, and smoothing with an ivory or agate burnisher.

BARGE BOARD.

BUTTRESS.—If they are to a large scale, say quarter-inch, one foot, they are best boxed out; the angles carefully and accurately mitred. Less scale, they may be boxed out of double thickness, as described for chimney shafts; or, if very small size, they may be cut from the solid.

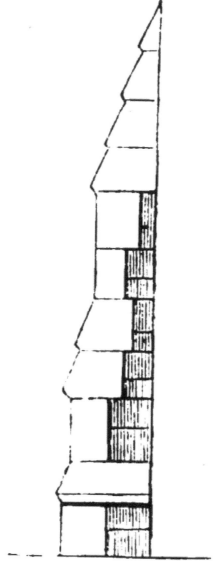

SIDE VIEW.

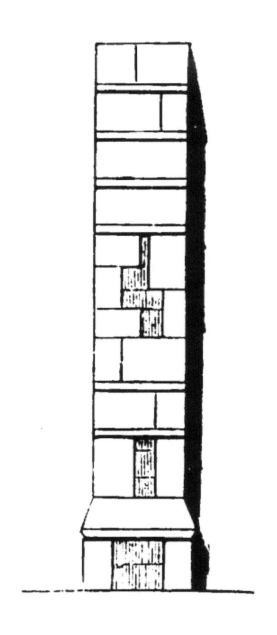

FRONT VIEW.

BALUSTRADE.—Model the capping as described for cornices, with the exception, this will be worked upon both faces.

BLOCKING.—To a cornice. This, if large, is best constructed by being boxed out. If small in size, cut them out of the solid.

BRACKET.—Brackets in Gothic work are to be constructed in layers, in a similar manner as described for cornices; other brackets may be cut from the solid paper, first by making a pattern, or template, in thin tea lead, or sheet copper, and marking round the edge upon the paper, uniformity of size being thus ensured.

C.

CORNICES.—The construction of cornices is fully described in that of the House, illustrated, and also under the head of Arch, where a cornice is described as illustrating the formation of moulded arches.

COINS, or QUOINS; see those described for House, page 64, *ante*; also Ashlar-work.

COPING.—If the coping be small scale, cut from the solid by the adjusting straight-edge; otherwise they are better boxed out.

CRESTING.—Proceed in much the same manner as described for barge boards; use a template to save trouble in pencilling out, and cut with knife No. 3; three thicknesses are ample for eighth scale work.

CUSPS.—See description of Tracery; window-cusps being circular work, No. 3 knife must be used.

CORBEL.—Refer to Cantilevers in House Tower Cornice, the method of modelling being the same, except such as are composed of a series of horizontal mouldings, in which case proceed as for cornices.

CONSOLE.—The console given for example is composed vertically of five separate pieces; horizontally of two, each separate part receiving its proper form, and when completed, gummed together.

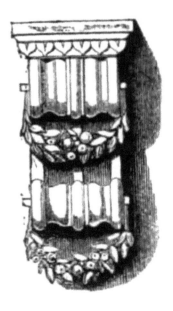 

CAPITAL, CORINTHIAN.—We choose for illustrating the method adopted for modelling capitals, a Corinthian one, as most useful for our purpose. The example given is from the Temple of Vesta, at Tivoli, a beautiful and peculiar example, to model which proceed thus

A A A Flowers in the abacus.   1 2 3 Abacus.   B B Volutes.   C C Caulicoles.   C* Bell.   1 2 3 Astragal.   D D D Flutes.

Compose the abacus of three layers, 1, ovolo, 2, fillet, 3, cyma; then the bell of the capital must be turned out of some close-grained wood, and attached to the astragal, composed of three pieces, 1, fillet, 2, astragal, 3, fillet. The leaves are then to be modelled, as described under the head of ornaments, also the flower in the abacus; the volutes and caulicoles in a similar manner to that described for consoles. When all are prepared, they must be fixed most accurately in their places. The bell of the capital must be tinted previously, to resemble in colour the rest of the work.

COLUMN, CIRCULAR.—This description of columns must be formed out of very thin paper, rolled as close as possible to the required lengths and diameters, thinning the paper at the extreme edge with a very sharp knife to conceal the join. If the columns are too small to be cleverly rolled, they may be turned as described for balusters; should the columns (as in classic work,) diminish, then procure a wood core to roll the paper round, and when the paper is gummed and dry, withdraw the core. It will now be obvious that combinations of various descriptions occurring so frequently in Gothic work, may easily be represented as this column in plan, being nothing more than four rolls joined together. If the columns are too small for paper, turn shafts, bases, and caps at once; by this means much unnecessary trouble will be saved, and a superior effect produced.

D.

DENTILS.—Model dentils in the same manner as previously described for brackets, cantilevers, &c.

DOME.—Whatever the shape of the dome you wish to model may be, a pattern on which to form it had best be turned in wood; this forms a basis upon which the paper casing may remain until dry, and then the mould may be removed. It has not been thought necessary within the limits of this work to include the development of the various shapes of domes and cupolas, the student being deemed master of this branch of science. If, however, he should not be, any work on practical geometry will supply his wants.

DOORS.—A copious description of the manner of modelling doors is given in those described for the House, page 51, *ante.*

F.

FLUTES.—In order to flute a column, we proceed thus: first roll the column up as before described, taking care to have it smaller than if plain, to allow the fluted piece to make up the required diameter; then prepare a piece of paper (one thickness will do), cut it of sufficient size to go once round the column, and join exactly; upon this piece carefully space or mark out the divisions of the flutings. Now procure a piece of soft straight-grained *deal*, perfectly free from knots, and with some blunt, round-headed instrument (one of the modelling tools, or a piece of ivory filed smooth,) indent the wood with a groove the exact length of the required flute, upon which (the paper having been previously *damped* only), press it into the wood groove all along the flute with the same tool the groove was made with, and so proceed with each in succession, gumming them to the column when dry.

H.

HOLLOWS.—In forming hollows in mouldings, &c., if large, proceed as described under the head of Arch; if small, first cut by means of the "adjusting straight-edge," an angle, thus, **V**; and then with a curved ivory tool give it the required concavity by pressure along the whole length of the previously cut angle.

HOOD MOULD.—These may be cut with the "knife-compass," and the mouldings worked by fitting a piece of ivory filed to the required form in lieu of the knife; they must be slightly gummed upon the underside to the cutting-board, to keep them steady while being worked.

I.

IRONWORK.—May be represented in either paper, tea-lead, thin sheet copper, or wire, depending on size and form; perhaps the easiest and best material for general purposes is tea-lead, *i. e.*, the lead with which the tea chests are lined.

O.

ORNAMENTS.—Under this head is included every description of foliage, leaves, &c. All the leaves, &c., must be carefully drawn and cut out, and then indented on either side, as concavity or convexity is desired, in a similar manner to the operation of fluting a column, with the different *ivory* modelling tools on a piece of soft yielding deal. Bosses, crocketts, finials, festoons, wreaths, in short every description of foliage, and even sculpture in bas-relief, may be beautifully modelled by these simple means.

T.

TRACERY WINDOW.—The general method of modelling windows of this description is very simple, but the practice difficult. First, paper upon which you intend to cut out any tracery, must be *pressed* closer together than that used for ordinary work, so as to afford more assistance to the knife when cutting on the splay. Having drawn the design of your window, proceed to cut out all the interstices with knife No. 3; then splay down from the nosing with knives Nos. 1 and 2, as each may be found useful, cutting through with one stroke, or rather with a succession of short strokes right through on the slant, boldly and without leaving a jagged edge; afterwards smooth your work with ivory or agate. You had better place the pieces that came from between the mullions while cutting the splay, in their places again between the mullions, to offer resistance to the knife and prevent them bending. The eyes may be successfully formed by packing-needles of diamond shape, fixed in a handle.

END OF THE GLOSSARY.

TO THE READER.

It will have afforded the Author sincere gratification if the contents of this little work have found favour in the eyes of the Reader, and have been a ready help to him in his efforts in Architectural Modelling. Next to the pleasure of learning, is that of imparting knowledge. The Author has endeavoured, to the best of his ability, to render all his instructions clear and practical, at the same time divesting them of all unnecessary technicalities, and rendering them as terse as possible.

FINIS.

Ingram Content Group UK Ltd.
Milton Keynes UK
UKHW012022190623
423702UK00006B/768